Group's

BIBLE SENSE™

JAMES

// SHOWING OUR FAITH IN JESUS

Group
Loveland, Colorado
www.group.com

Group resources actually work!

This Group resource helps you focus on **"The 1 Thing®"**— a life-changing relationship with Jesus Christ. "The 1 Thing" incorporates our **R.E.A.L.** approach to ministry. It reinforces a growing friendship with Jesus, encourages long-term learning, and results in life transformation, because it's:

Relational
Learner-to-learner interaction enhances learning and builds Christian friendships.

Experiential
What learners experience through discussion and action sticks with them up to 9 times longer than what they simply hear or read.

Applicable
The aim of Christian education is to equip learners to be both hearers and doers of God's Word.

Learner-based
Learners understand and retain more when the learning process takes into consideration how they learn best.

Group's BIBLESENSE™
JAMES: Showing Our Faith in Jesus
Copyright © 2006 Group Publishing, Inc.

Visit our Web site: **www.group.com**

Credits
Contributors: A. Koshy Muthalaly, David Trujillo, Kelli B. Trujillo, Roxanne Wieman, Jeff White, and Paul Woods
Editor: Carl Simmons
Creative Development Editor: Matt Lockhart
Chief Creative Officer: Joani Schultz
Copy Editor: Lyndsay Gerwing
Senior Designer: Kari K. Monson
Cover Art Director: Jeff A. Storm
Cover Designer: Andrea Filer
Photographer: Rodney Stewart
Production Manager: DeAnne Lear

Unless otherwise indicated, all Scripture quotations are taken from the *Holy Bible,* New Living Translation, copyright © 1996, 2004. Used by permission of Tyndale House Publishers, Inc., Wheaton, Illinois 60189. All rights reserved.

Library of Congress Cataloging-in-Publication Data
James : showing our faith in Jesus.-- 1st American pbk. ed.
   p. cm. -- (Group's BibleSense)
Includes bibliographical references.
 ISBN-13: 978-0-7644-3242-2 (pbk. : alk. paper)
 1. Bible. N.T. James--Study and teaching. 2. Bible. N.T.
James--Criticism, interpretation, etc. I. Group Publishing. II. Series.
 BS2785.55.J36 2006
 227'.910071--dc22
             2006008358
ISBN: 0-7644-3242-7

10 9 8 7 6 5 4 3 2 1   15 14 13 12 11 10 09 08 07 06
Printed in the United States of America.

CONTENTS

CONTENTS CONTINUED

INTRODUCTION

TO GROUP'S BIBLESENSE™

Welcome to **Group's BibleSense**™, a book-of-the-Bible series unlike any you've ever seen! This is a Bible study series in which you'll literally be able to *see, hear, smell, taste, and touch God's Word*—not only through seeing and hearing the actual book of the Bible you're studying on DVD but also through thought-provoking questions and group activities. As you do these sessions, you'll bring the Word to life, bring your group closer together as a community, and help your group members bring that life to others.

Whether you're new to small groups or have been doing them for years, you'll discover new, exciting, and—dare we say it—*fun* ways to learn and apply God's Word to your life in these sessions. And as you dig deeper into the Bible passage for each session and its meaning for your life, you'll find your life (and the lives around you) transformed more and more into Jesus' likeness.

Each session concludes with a series of opportunities on how to commit to reaching your world with the Bible passage you've just studied—whether it's in changing your own responses to others, in reaching out to them individually or as an entire group, or by taking part in something bigger than your group.

So again, welcome to the world of BibleSense! We hope that you'll find the experiences and studies here both meaningful and memorable and that as you do them together, your lives will grow even more into the likeness of our Lord, Jesus Christ.

—Carl Simmons, Editor

ABOUT THE SESSIONS

TASTE AND SEE (20 minutes)

Every BibleSense session begins with food—to give group members a chance to unwind and transition from a busy day and other preoccupations into the theme of the session. After the food and a few introductory questions, the group gets to experience Scripture in a fresh way. The passage for each session is included on DVD, as well as in print within the book. Also provided is "A Sense of History," a brief feature offering additional cultural and historical context.

DIGGING INTO SCRIPTURE (30 minutes)

This is the central part of the session. The group will have the chance to interact with the Scripture passage you've just read and watched, and, through questions and other sensory experiences, you'll learn how it applies to *your* life.

MAKING IT PERSONAL (15 minutes)

Now you'll move from understanding *how* the passage applies to your life to thinking about ways you *can* apply it. In this part of the session, personal meaning is brought home through meaningful experiences and questions.

TOUCHING YOUR WORLD (25 minutes)

This is the "take home" part of the session. Each group member will choose a weekly challenge to directly apply this session's passage in a practical way in the week ahead, as well as share prayer requests and pray for one another. Also included is a "Taking It Home" section with tips on how you can prepare for your next session.

GETTING CONNECTED

Pass your books around the room, and have group members write their names, phone numbers, e-mail addresses, and birthdays.

Name	Phone	E-mail	Birthday

SESSION 1:

PUSHING FORWARD IN JESUS

JAMES 1:1-18

In this session you'll learn how to stay encouraged and keep your perspective on Jesus, even in tough times.

PRE-SESSION CHECKLIST:

☐ **Leader:** Check out the Session 1 Leader Notes in the back of the book (p. 91).

☐ **Food Coordinator:** If you are responsible for the Session 1 snack, see page 103.

☐ **Supplies:**

- binoculars—if possible, a pair for everyone in the group

TASTE AND SEE (20 minutes)

While enjoying the snack, find a partner—someone you don't know very well—
and take a few minutes to tell your partner a couple of things about yourself:

- Where did you grow up?

Write it down!
Pass your books around to record each other's contact information (p. 7).

- Thinking back to your childhood, who do you remember
  being your best neighbors? What made them stand out?

- What's the nicest thing a neighbor has ever done for you?

Gather back together as a large group. Take turns introducing your partner to
the group by sharing one thing you learned about him or her that you didn't already
know. Choose one of the following questions to answer and share with the group.

- Which of the two snacks did you choose? Do you usually prefer sweet or
  sour snacks?

Did you know? *Like
sweets? So does the tip
of your tongue! The taste
buds most sensitive to
detecting sweetness are
on the tongue's tip; those
that detect sour flavors
best are on the sides of
your tongue.*

- When has someone shared a "sweet"—*or* "sour"—word
  that helped you recently?

Watch the first chapter on the DVD (James
1:1-18). This passage can also be found on the
following page if you would like to follow along in
your book.

James 1:1-18

¹This letter is from James, a slave of God and of the Lord Jesus Christ.

I am writing to the "twelve tribes"—Jewish believers scattered abroad.

Greetings!

²Dear brothers and sisters, when troubles come your way, consider it an opportunity for great joy. ³For you know that when your faith is tested, your endurance has a chance to grow. ⁴So let it grow, for when your endurance is fully developed, you will be perfect and complete, needing nothing.

⁵If you need wisdom, ask our generous God, and he will give it to you. He will not rebuke you for asking. ⁶But when you ask him, be sure that your faith is in God alone. Do not waver, for a person with divided loyalty is as unsettled as a wave of the sea that is blown and tossed by the wind. ⁷Such people should not expect to receive anything from the Lord. ⁸Their loyalty is divided between God and the world, and they are unstable in everything they do.

⁹Believers who are poor have something to boast about, for God has honored them. ¹⁰And those who are rich should boast that God has humbled them. They will fade away like a little flower in the field. ¹¹The hot sun rises and the grass withers; the little flower droops and falls, and its beauty fades away. In the same way, the rich will fade away with all of their achievements.

¹²God blesses those who patiently endure testing and temptation. Afterward they will receive the crown of life that God has promised to those who love him. ¹³And remember, when you are being tempted, do not say, "God is tempting me." God is never tempted to do wrong, and he never tempts anyone else. ¹⁴Temptation comes from our own desires, which entice us and drag us away. ¹⁵These desires give birth to sinful actions. And when sin is allowed to grow, it gives birth to death.

¹⁶So don't be misled, my dear brothers and sisters. ¹⁷Whatever is good and perfect comes down to us from God our Father, who created all the lights in the heavens. He never changes or casts a shifting shadow. ¹⁸He chose to give birth to us by giving us his true word. And we, out of all creation, became his prized possession.

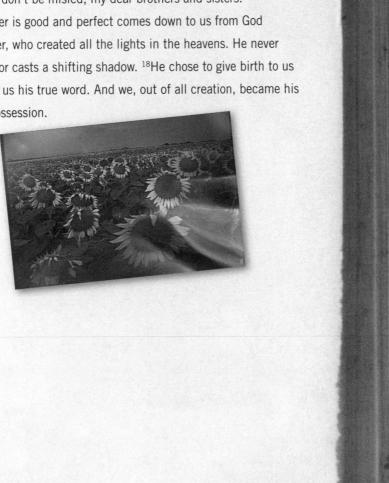

DIGGING INTO SCRIPTURE (30 minutes)

As a group, discuss:

• What thoughts or emotions came to your mind while watching this session's Bible passage?

Tip: To maximize participation and also to have enough time to work through the session, we recommend breaking into smaller subgroups of three or four at various points during the session.

Now break into subgroups.

Subgroup Leaders: Find a place where your subgroup can talk with few distractions. Plan to come back together in 15 minutes.

In your subgroup read James 1:1-18 and the following "A Sense of History" feature, and answer the questions that follow.

A SENSE OF HISTORY

James and the Jerusalem Church

It is generally believed that the author of this letter was James, the half-brother of Jesus, who became the acknowledged leader of the early Jerusalem church. The letter is addressed to the "twelve tribes," suggesting that James was writing to Jewish Christians. Written in response to this early persecution in Judea, the book of James addresses many Christians who were forced outside of Palestine to the north and west.

These early Jewish Christians who were compelled to flee from their homes experienced two kinds of misery. First, their displacement, no doubt, resulted in poverty. Second, the trials and persecution they experienced in Jerusalem seem to have followed them. Thus, James begins his letter by reminding these Jewish Christians, "When troubles come your way, consider it an opportunity for great joy."

• Which of the troubles or tough circumstances you just read about seem the worst to you? Why?

• What specific things does James encourage his readers to do in response to these circumstances?

• What do all these encouragements have in common?

Come back together as a larger group, and share any highlights or questions from your subgroup discussion.

Leader: Give the pairs of binoculars to your group members.

> **Did you know?**
> Many scholars believe James actually coined the word translated here as "loyalty...divided" in verse 8. The original Greek word is dipsychos, and its literal translation is "double-souled." James uses this word again in James 4:8 when he describes his readers' wavering commitment to their faith.

Take your binoculars, and go outside (or to a window). Take turns using the binoculars to look at distant objects: stars, lights, buildings, cars, trees, hills.

After everyone has had a turn, sit back down as a larger group and answer the following questions:

• Think about the different perspective the binoculars gave you. What details did you notice that you wouldn't have ordinarily?

• Why is a *God*-focused perspective so important for people going through trials?

• When has a change of perspective helped you get through a trial or tough time? What caused that change, and how did it affect you?

MAKING IT PERSONAL (15 minutes)

Read James 1:2-15 one more time, and answer the following:

• How are the circumstances of the original recipients of James' letter different from your own? How are they similar?

• Which of James' words—the sweet or the sour—do you most need to hear and apply to your own life right now?

> **Did you know?**
> Many Christians today face terrible persecution much like the early church. Find out more about how you can help by visiting Voice of the Martyrs' Web site: www.persecution.com.

• What's one way you can be a James to others, sharing the sweet or sour words they need to hear to keep pushing forward in Jesus?

TOUCHING YOUR WORLD (25 minutes)

Review the following "weekly challenge" options, and select the challenge you'd like to do. Turn to a partner, and share your choice. Then make plans to connect with your partner sometime between now and the next session to check in with and encourage one another.

☐ **WRITE A LETTER OF ENCOURAGEMENT.** Look around you. Who could benefit from some words of encouragement right now? Block out an hour, and be intentional about writing a letter of encouragement to him or her. Pray and seek God's guidance. You could even write your letter by hand and send it by regular mail to add a personal touch.

☐ **LET YOURSELF BE CHALLENGED.** Change your perspective. Ask someone to be a James to you. Invite him or her to point out areas in which you need to grow. Even if the words hurt at first, thank the person for his or her input. Pray about the growth areas he or she pointed out, and identify ways you can grow in those areas.

☐ **"ADOPT" A GROUP OF PERSECUTED CHRISTIANS.** Search the Internet, talk to missionaries, and read up on the persecuted church today. Identify a specific group of Christians somewhere in the world who face persecution for their faith, and then do what you can to support them through regular prayer and other practical ideas.

☐ **HELP OTHERS MEET CHALLENGES.** Think of someone in your neighborhood or elsewhere who's facing a tough time right now, and then commit to helping him or her. If it's something that can be done as a group, give your group's outreach coordinator ideas on who you want to reach out to and how so he or she can plan an event.

Come back together as a group. Share prayer requests. Before the leader prays, take a few moments to be silent and appreciate God's goodness and ability to meet all the needs in your life.

Leader: If you haven't already, take a few minutes to review the group roles and assignments (p. 100) with the group. At minimum, be sure that the food and supplies responsibilities for the next session are covered.

Until next time...

 Date _____

Time _____

Place _____

Taking It Home:

1. Set a goal for how many times you'll either read through or watch on your DVD the Session 2 Bible passage (James 1:19-27). Make a point to read the "Sense of History" feature in Session 2 (p. 21) prior to the next session. You may want to review this week's passage as well. Let your weekly challenge partner know what goals you've set so he or she can encourage you and help hold you accountable.

2. Touch base sometime before the next session with your weekly challenge partner to compare notes on how you're both doing with the goals you've set.

3. If you have volunteered for a role or signed up to help with food or supplies for the next session, be sure to prepare for this. The Session 2 supplies list can be found on page 18, and the Food Coordinator instructions are on page 103.

4. **I commit to touching my world this week by pushing forward in my walk with Jesus in the following ways:**

_____

_____

_____

SESSION 2:

REMEMBERING YOUR REFLECTION

JAMES 1:19-27

In this session you'll discover how to remember—and show others—who you are in Jesus.

PRE-SESSION CHECKLIST:

☐ **Leader:** Check out the Session 2 Leader Notes in the back of the book (p. 92).

☐ **Food Coordinator:** If you are responsible for the Session 2 snack, see page 103.

☐ **Supplies:**

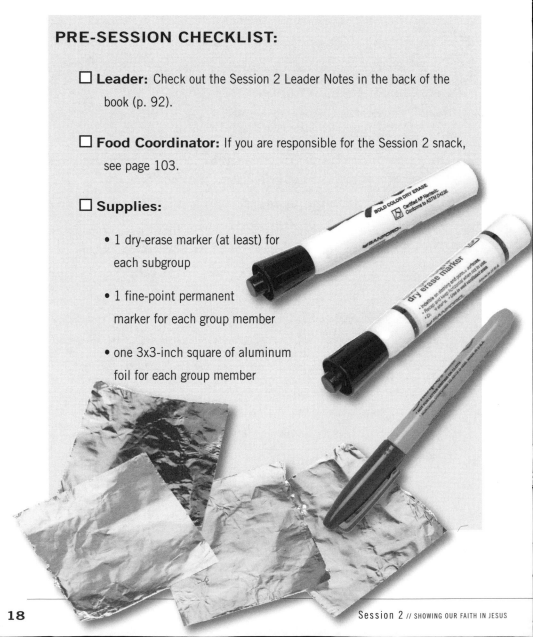

- 1 dry-erase marker (at least) for each subgroup

- 1 fine-point permanent marker for each group member

- one 3x3-inch square of aluminum foil for each group member

TASTE AND SEE (20 minutes)

Put your inner artist to work. Use a bagel half and other snack supplies to create a self-portrait. Use the veggies and other toppings to represent your hair, eyes, nose, mouth, and other features. Be creative.

> **Extra Impact:** *To add a twist to this activity, create your snack self-portraits in private, without letting others see. Your Food Coordinator can collect all the bagels and arrange them on a center table, and then everyone can gather around and guess who each self-portrait represents.*

Before you eat your self-portrait—or any other food—show your "face" to the rest of the group. Take a poll on whose self-portrait most closely represents his or her real appearance, and give a round of applause!

While you eat, discuss the following:

• Was it easy or tough to create a representation of yourself? Why?

• How accurately did your bagel-face mirror your real appearance? Were others able to recognize the resemblance?

 Watch the second chapter on the DVD (James 1:19-27). This passage can also be found on the following page if you would like to follow along in your book.

James 1:19-27

[19]Understand this, my dear brothers and sisters: You must all be quick to listen, slow to speak, and slow to get angry. [20]Human anger does not produce the righteousness God desires. [21]So get rid of all the filth and evil in your lives, and humbly accept the word God has planted in your hearts, for it has the power to save your souls.

[22]But don't just listen to God's word. You must do what it says. Otherwise, you are only fooling yourselves. [23]For if you listen to the word and don't obey, it is like glancing at your face in a mirror. [24]You see yourself, walk away, and forget what you look like. [25]But if you look carefully into the perfect law that sets you free, and if you do what it says and don't forget what you heard, then God will bless you for doing it.

[26]If you claim to be religious but don't control your tongue, you are fooling yourself, and your religion is worthless. [27]Pure and genuine religion in the sight of God the Father means caring for orphans and widows in their distress and refusing to let the world corrupt you.

A SENSE OF HISTORY

"Pure and Genuine Religion," Then and Now

The principles in James 1:19-27, especially verse 27, must be viewed in light of Old Testament history. Throughout the Old Testament, the helpless of society were the orphans, widows, and aliens. Each of these groups was in a vulnerable position—when anyone took interest in them at all, it was usually to take advantage of their plight. In fact, conditions were so polarized that God accused the wealthy of *trampling* the poor (Amos 2:7; 5:11; 8:4).

The height of this oppression came during the reigns of Jeroboam II in Israel and Amaziah in Judah during the 8th century B.C. Historian John Bright writes, "The system, which was itself harsh, was made harsher by the greed of the wealthy, who took unmerciful advantage of the plight of the poor...[through] the falsification of weights and measures, and various legal dodges." And because the system was corrupt, "the poor had no redress."

God thundered his response through the prophet Amos: "I want to see a mighty flood of justice, an endless river of righteous living" (Amos 5:24). God delivered a similar message to Judah through Isaiah: "As for your celebrations of the new moon and the Sabbath and your special days for fasting—they are all sinful and false. I want no more of your pious meetings. I hate your new moon celebrations and your annual festivals. They are a burden to me. I cannot stand them! When you lift up your hands in prayer, I will not look...Learn to do good. Seek justice. Help the oppressed. Defend the cause of orphans. Fight for the rights of widows" (Isaiah 1:13-15, 17).

Some 800 years later, God uses James to remind his people of this same truth. James sees the pattern of neglecting the poor once again emerge among God's people, and he sees works—looking after the helpless—as the mark of true worship and, hence, as the evidence of genuine faith.

DIGGING INTO SCRIPTURE (30 minutes)

As a group, discuss:

• What thoughts or emotions came to your mind while watching this session's Bible passage, whether just now or during the past week?

Now break into subgroups.

Subgroup Leaders: Find a place where your subgroup can talk with few distractions. Take no more than 15 minutes for your discussion time.

Read James 1:19-27 together, and answer the following questions:

• What characteristics of a true Christian does James mention here?

> **Did you know?**
> Thirty-seven million Americans live below the poverty line ($9,570 for a single person; $19,350 for a family of four).
> (U.S. Census poverty report, 2005)

• How does the analogy of the person looking into the mirror relate to these characteristics?

• How does James' definition of "pure and genuine religion" compare or contrast with the way most Christians practice their faith today? with *your own* faith and daily living?

Come back together as a larger group, and share your answers with one another.

Break back into subgroups.

Leader: Give each subgroup a dry-erase marker, and direct subgroups to the rooms you have prepared.

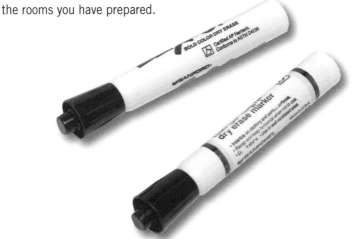

In your subgroup, take turns using the marker to write on the mirror the traits James identified as marks of a true Jesus-follower. Add other traits emphasized in Scripture or other characteristics of following Jesus you know are important. Don't be shy—write *large*.

Subgroup Leaders (and Leader): Don't worry—it erases!

Gather in front of the mirror so you all can see your reflections. One person at a time, underline a trait on the mirror that you feel is a strength in your life or an area in which you regularly express your faith.

Now get tough on yourself. Which of the traits on the mirror is *not* reflected well in your life? Take a turn circling a weakness in your life—an area in which you know you need to do a better job of putting those traits into practice.

> **Fast fact:**
> *Archaeologists believe the earliest mirrors were small hand mirrors made out of convex discs of pounded metal. The first large mirrors, in which a person could see his entire body, are thought to have been first used during the 1st century A.D., when James wrote this letter.*

When everyone has finished, sit back down in your subgroups and answer the following questions:

• What's your reaction to seeing your strengths *and* your weaknesses in the mirror?

• How would you like to change your "face," now that you've seen it up close?

Read James 1:19-27 again, and answer the following:
• How has your look into the "mirror" of God's Word in James changed your way of seeing your life and faith in Jesus?

Come back together as a larger group, and share your answers with one another.

MAKING IT PERSONAL (15 minutes)

In the large group, answer the following question:

• Which of James' two "bookends"—righteousness toward God or service to those in need—do you most need to work on? Explain.

Leader: Give out the aluminum squares of foil and fine-point permanent markers.

Use your marker to write on your square of foil a word or phrase that represents one specific thing you want to remember and apply to your life from this session.

When you've finished, break into pairs. Show your foil square to your partner, and discuss the following:

• How has God been speaking to you about the issue you wrote down?

• What's one thing you'll do to make what you wrote down a reality in your life?

Staying in your pairs, go directly to "Touching Your World."

> **On your own time:**
> James' emphasis on remembering was also a bedrock principle of the Old Testament. Check out these Scriptures on the importance of remembering spiritual truths: Deuteronomy 8:2, 11, 14, 18, and 19.

TOUCHING YOUR WORLD (25 minutes)

Review the following "weekly challenge" options, and select the challenge you'd like to do. Turn to a partner, and share your choice. Then make plans to connect with your partner sometime between now and the next session to check in with and encourage one another.

☐ **INTERVIEW A NON-CHRISTIAN FRIEND.** Get his or her perspective on what he or she thinks Christians are "really" like. Don't come with an agenda—just listen. Use this as an opportunity to hear some of the stereotypes about Christians and to understand why your friend has these perceptions. Ask God to give you insight into how *your* life can best represent Christ's mission and values.

☐ **KEEP A "REMEMBRANCE" JOURNAL THIS WEEK.** How have you followed through on the commitment you made on your piece of foil? Daily, write at least one specific way you applied it to your life. Share your daily record with an accountability partner and/or your pair-share partner.

☐ **COMPOSE A PERSONAL PRAYER.** Write on your bathroom mirror a prayer in response to James 1:19-27. (Again, use a dry-erase marker—it will wipe right off.) Pray through it daily, asking God to change you and make you more like Christ.

☐ **AS A GROUP, IDENTIFY "THE HELPLESS"** in your immediate circle of contact, and create a plan for helping them. Pray for God's guidance concerning how he wants you to get involved in helping the helpless. Consider your passions, your availability, and your location. Work together to identify a practical, meaningful way you can help, and then get to it.

Come back together as a group. Share prayer requests, and then pray for everyone's needs. Take time to go around the room and recognize how each person reflects Jesus in his or her life and pray that God would show him or her even more ways to do that.

Until next time...

Date _____

Time _____

Place _____

Taking It Home:

1. Set a goal for how many times you'll either read through or watch on your DVD the Session 3 Bible passage (James 2:1-13). Make a point to read the "Sense of History" feature in Session 3 (p. 31) before the next session. You may want to review this week's passage as well—or even watch the entire book of James straight through. (It takes about 16 minutes.) Let your weekly challenge partner know what goals you've set so he or she can encourage you and help hold you accountable.

2. Touch base sometime before the next session with your weekly challenge partner to compare notes on how you're both doing with the goals you've set.

3. If you have volunteered for a role or signed up to help with food or supplies for the next session, be sure to prepare for this. The Session 3 supplies list can be found on page 28, and the Food Coordinator instructions are on page 104.

4. **I commit to touching my world this week by remembering who I am in Jesus in the following ways:**

_____

_____

_____

_____

SESSION 3:

PRIDE AND PREJUDICE

JAMES 2:1-13

In this session you'll examine the peril of prejudice and how to better "love your neighbor as yourself."

PRE-SESSION CHECKLIST:

☐ **Leader:** Check out the Session 3 Leader Notes in the back of the book (p. 93).

☐ **Food Coordinator:** If you are responsible for the Session 3 snack, see page 104.

☐ **Supplies:**

- 1 envelope for each person in the group

- 1 paper scrap (to write on) for each person in the group

- 1 pen or pencil for each person in the group

- 1 small bowl

TASTE AND SEE (20 minutes)

For this session, you have your choice of an assortment of foods from a variety of cultures. Take whatever you like!

While you're enjoying your snack, discuss the following:

• Which foods did you choose? Why?

Once everyone has finished his or her snack, go back to the snack table and bring back the item you *disliked* the most, even if you didn't taste it. Discuss the following questions:

• Which snack did you choose—or, in this case, reject?

• Did you try it? If not, why did you reject it before you tried it?

 Watch the third chapter on the DVD (James 2:1-13). This passage can also be found on the following page.

James 2:1-13

[1]My dear brothers and sisters, how can you claim to have faith in our glorious Lord Jesus Christ if you favor some people over others?

[2]For example, suppose someone comes into your meeting dressed in fancy clothes and expensive jewelry, and another comes in who is poor and dressed in dirty clothes. [3]If you give special attention and a good seat to the rich person, but you say to the poor one, "You can stand over there, or else sit on the floor"— well, [4]doesn't this discrimination show that your judgments are guided by evil motives?

[5]Listen to me, dear brothers and sisters. Hasn't God chosen the poor in this world to be rich in faith? Aren't they the ones who will inherit the Kingdom he promised to those who love him? [6]But you dishonor the poor! Isn't it the rich who oppress you and drag you into court? [7]Aren't they the ones who slander Jesus Christ, whose noble name you bear?

[8]Yes indeed, it is good when you obey the royal law as found in the Scriptures: "Love your neighbor as yourself." [9]But if you favor some people over others, you are committing a sin. You are guilty of breaking the law.

[10]For the person who keeps all of the laws except one is as guilty as a person who has broken all of God's laws. [11]For the same God who said, "You

must not commit adultery," also said, "You must not murder." So if you murder someone but do not commit adultery, you have still broken the law.

¹²So whatever you say or whatever you do, remember that you will be judged by the law that sets you free. ¹³There will be no mercy for those who have not shown mercy to others. But if you have been merciful, God will be merciful when he judges you.

A SENSE OF HISTORY
Prejudice in James' Time

In biblical times, the Jews hated the Samaritans, and vice versa. They had their own separate places of worship and their own cultures. (An illustration of this is found in Jesus' conversation with the Samaritan woman at Jacob's well in John 4:19-24.) By the same token, there was almost constant conflict in the Bible between the Jews, who called themselves the "children of Abraham," and those who were not Jews. The latter were called the Gentiles.

And there was always the division between the rich and the poor. Most people in James' day were agrarian by lifestyle. Jesus himself used many illustrations in his teaching about those who were hired workers on the land (Matthew 20:1-16 and Luke 10:1-3 are two such examples). The rich were the landowners who hired the poor to work in their fields for long hours and paid them low wages for their work. The pride of the rich caused them to indulge in their lavish lifestyles while the poor suffered all around them.

James insists on a common idea of community in the kingdom of those who believe in the same Lord Jesus. The servants of Christ are called to share all their earthly resources with others in their need (Acts 2:43-47; 1 Timothy 5). In this lies the essence of the Christian faith.

DIGGING INTO SCRIPTURE (30 minutes)

As a group, discuss:

• What thoughts or emotions came to your mind while watching this session's Bible passage, whether just now or during the past week?

Now break into subgroups.

Subgroup Leaders: Find a place where your subgroup can talk with few distractions. Take up to 15 minutes for your discussion time.

"Prejudice: *A hostile opinion about some person or class of persons. Prejudice is socially learned and is usually grounded in misconception, misunderstanding, and inflexible generalizations.*"

—The New Dictionary of Cultural Literacy, *Third Edition, 2002*

Read James 2:1-13, and answer the following questions:

• Think about the food you rejected earlier. How is this similar to the way we approach people who are different from us? How is it different?

• How do appearances affect our reactions to people? What does this tell us about our own "wrong motives"?

• What different people, or groups of people, have you had problems connecting with in the past? Why?

Come back together as a larger group, and share any highlights or questions from your subgroup discussion.

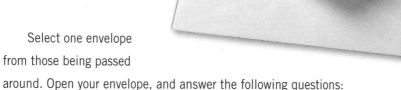

Leader: Pass the envelopes around the room.

Select one envelope from those being passed around. Open your envelope, and answer the following questions:

- What was your initial reaction toward the picture you found in your envelope? Is this person someone you'd invite to dinner if you had the chance? Why or why not?

- How do we play favorites with those who are more influential or to whom we're more naturally drawn?

> "*The very ink with which history is written is merely fluid prejudice.*"
> —*Mark Twain*

- How did your reactions line up with what James teaches us in this passage? What does this suggest about wrong motives that *we* might be harboring?

MAKING IT PERSONAL (15 minutes)

Leader: Grab your bowl for this activity. Give everyone paper scraps, and make sure each person has a pen or pencil.

Think of a time you felt discriminated against or judged by others around you, for whatever reason. On your paper scrap, write a word or a phrase describing what that experience felt like. Then fold up your scrap, and place it in the bowl as it's passed around.

Pass the bowl around again. This time, everyone take out a scrap. Read your scrap aloud, and listen as others read their scraps. Then answer the following questions:

- How did it feel to read aloud the scrap you took? How did it feel to have the scrap you put in read aloud?

- What does this tell you about the damage that's done when people are discriminated against or judged by others?

- How can you train yourself to see past appearances and see those people as Jesus would?

TOUCHING YOUR WORLD (25 minutes)

Review the following "weekly challenge" options, and select the challenge you'd like to do. Turn to a partner, and share your choice. Then make plans to connect with your partner sometime between now and the next session to check in with and encourage one another.

☐ **ASSESS YOUR OWN PREJUDICES.** Set aside time this week to write down some of the prejudices you have identified in your life. Once you've done that, set a goal to address those prejudices. Commit these issues to God, and commit to praying that God will address these issues and any related ones in your life.

☐ **VISIT AND MAKE FRIENDS** with a neighbor who does not belong to your social or economic class, religion, or race. Afterward, write down some of the things you experienced during your visit. How did the experience change your perceptions? How will it change how you approach your neighbors (and others of their class, belief, or race) in the future?

☐ **PRAY FOR UNREACHED PEOPLE GROUPS** all over the world. According to the Joshua Project (www.joshuaproject.net), there still are more than 6,000 "ethno-linguistic" groups around the world that have not yet heard the good news of Jesus Christ. Many of these groups are quite small (fewer than 10,000), but the fact is, Jesus died for all of them. Commit to praying that the Great Commission of making "disciples of all the nations" (Matthew 28:19) is fulfilled quickly.

☐ **REACH OUT AS A GROUP** to a family in need in the neighborhood or community who is of a different race or class from that which you're familiar. Maybe you can find an international family who is in need and take specific steps to help them in their situation.

Come back together as a group. Share prayer requests, and then pray for everyone's needs. Let your Prayer Coordinator lead this time of prayer, especially for issues uncovered during your pair-share time.

Until next time...

Date _____

Time _____

Place _____

Taking It Home:

1. Set a goal for how many times you'll either read through or watch on your DVD the Session 4 Bible passage (James 2:14-26). Make a point to read the "Sense of History" feature in Session 4 (p. 41) before the next session. You may also want to review this week's passage as well—or even watch the entire book of James straight through. (It takes about 16 minutes.) Let your weekly challenge partner know what goals you've set so he or she can encourage you and help hold you accountable.

2. Touch base sometime before the next session with your weekly challenge partner to compare notes on how you're both doing with the goals you've set.

3. If you have volunteered for a role or signed up to help with food or supplies for the next session, be sure to prepare for this. The Session 4 supplies list can be found on page 38, and the Food Coordinator instructions are on page 104.

4. **I commit to touching my world this week by reaching out to others who are different from me in the following ways:**

_____

_____

_____

_____

SESSION 4:

TURNING FAITH INTO ACTION

JAMES 2:14-26

In this session you'll explore the importance of putting actions to your faith—and practical ways to do this!

PRE-SESSION CHECKLIST:

☐ **Leader:** Check out the Session 4 Leader Notes in the back of the book (p. 94).

☐ **Food Coordinator:** If you are responsible for the Session 4 snack, see page 104.

☐ **Supplies:**

- 1 houseplant in a 6-inch pot

- one 6-inch pot filled with soil and a seed that has not yet sprouted

- 1 pair of scissors

- 1 water-cooler-size cup for each person in the group

TASTE AND SEE (20 minutes)

While you're enjoying your snack, turn to a partner and share:

• What's one good thing you did this week? (That's right—go ahead and brag about yourself!)

• What's one good thing someone did for *you* this week?

Gather back together as a large group, and discuss the following:

• What was wrong with your snack tonight?

• What was your reaction when you took your first sip of soda?

 Watch the fourth chapter on the DVD (James 2:14-26).

James 2:14-26

14What good is it, dear brothers and sisters, if you say you have faith but don't show it by your actions? Can that kind of faith save anyone? 15Suppose you see a brother or sister who has no food or clothing, 16and you say, "Good-bye and have a good day; stay warm and eat well"—but then you don't give that person any food or clothing. What good does that do?

17So you see, faith by itself isn't enough. Unless it produces good deeds, it is dead and useless.

18Now someone may argue, "Some people have faith; others have good deeds." But I say, "How can you show me your faith if you don't have good deeds? I will show you my faith by my good deeds."

19You say you have faith, for you believe that there is one God. Good for you! Even the demons believe this, and they tremble in terror. 20How foolish! Can't you see that faith without good deeds is useless?

21Don't you remember that our ancestor Abraham was shown to be right with God by his actions when he offered his son Isaac on the altar? 22You see, his faith and his actions worked together. His actions made his faith complete. 23And so it happened just as the Scriptures say: "Abraham believed God, and God counted him as righteous because of his faith." He was even called the friend of God. 24So you see, we are shown to be right with God by what we do, not by faith alone.

25Rahab the prostitute is another example. She was shown to be right with God by her actions when she hid those messengers and sent them safely away by a different road. 26Just as the body is dead without breath, so also faith is dead without good works.

A SENSE OF HISTORY

Living Faith

The second chapter of James is a difficult one for many Christians—and not just because it's tough to live out. Even the great reformer Martin Luther struggled with it; he promised to give his doctor's cap to anyone who could show that James' teachings agreed with Paul's writings.

Here is an excerpt from Luther's preface to the book of James: "Firstly, because, in direct opposition to St. Paul and all the rest of the Bible, [James] ascribes justification to works, and declares that Abraham was justified by his works when he offered up his son. St. Paul, on the contrary, in Romans 4 [verse 3], teaches that Abraham was justified without works, by his faith alone, the proof being in Genesis 15 [verse 6], which was before he sacrificed his son."

Many Christians have come to terms with this chapter of James by understanding that James wasn't arguing for a works-based salvation—both Paul and James agreed that a man receives eternal life by faith. What James is arguing is this: *Genuine faith* produces fruit—good works—and Paul would agree with him on this. James is saying that a mere profession of faith does not guarantee possession of faith... because genuine faith can't sit by and do nothing when someone else is in need; genuine faith *must* act. Genuine faith changes a person, and the evidence of that change is a desire (and an action) to do good works. James concludes that workless faith is as empty as faithless works.

DIGGING INTO SCRIPTURE (30 minutes)

As a group, discuss:

• What thoughts or emotions came to your mind while watching this session's Bible passage?

Now break into subgroups.

Subgroup Leaders: Take no more than 20 minutes for your discussion time.

 Read James 2:14-26 in your subgroups, and answer the following questions:

• Think back to the soda you had with your snack, and then look at verse 17. What do you think of James' statement that faith without good deeds "is dead and useless"? Do you think that's completely true? Why or why not?

• What sort of acts would you consider to be proofs of someone's faith? Do you think it's even fair for someone to have to prove his or her faith? Why?

• Look at verse 19. When have you failed to back up your faith with actions? What reactions do you have hearing yourself be compared to demons who believe but don't act on their belief during those times?

• Based on this passage, what words would you use to describe your faith? Alive and kicking? A bit under the weather? Sick with the flu? Comatose? Explain your answer.

• According to James, what's the remedy for whatever spiritual-health issues we have? What might that look like in your life?

Come back together as a larger group, and share your thoughts with one another.

MAKING IT PERSONAL (15 minutes)

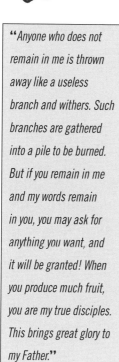

Leader: Set out the two pots, and have your scissors available.

> "Anyone who does not remain in me is thrown away like a useless branch and withers. Such branches are gathered into a pile to be burned. But if you remain in me and my words remain in you, you may ask for anything you want, and it will be granted! When you produce much fruit, you are my true disciples. This brings great glory to my Father."
>
> —John 15:6-8

Reread James 2:14-20 together. Look at the two pots in front of you. One holds a thriving plant; the other has a seed buried in the soil. Think of the plant as faith with good works and the seed as faith without good works. Answer the following:

- In what ways does this metaphor work? In what ways doesn't it work?

Leader: After discussing the first question, give a piece of the plant to each group member.

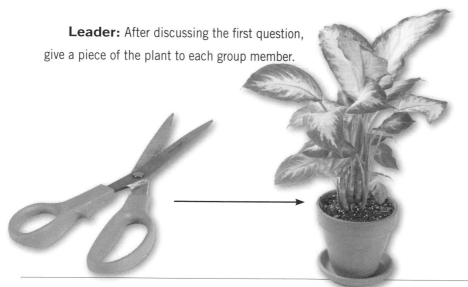

Answer the following questions:

• How is the part of the plant you're holding like works without faith? How isn't it?

• When have you tried to do good deeds without really being connected to your faith in Jesus? What was the result?

• What's one thing you can do to help keep your faith connected with your actions?

Keep your piece of the plant to take home with you as a reminder to keep your actions and faith connected.

Leader: Give a cup of water to each person in the group.

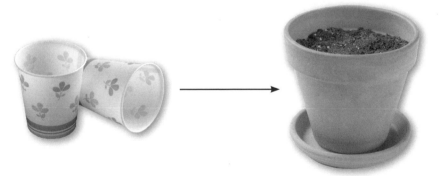

One at a time, pour your water into the pot with the seed in it. As you pour out your cup of water, briefly say aloud one way you can put your faith into action in the days to come. Examples: "I need to trust God to help me be more generous," "I need God's help in knowing how to volunteer in my community."

TOUCHING YOUR WORLD (25 minutes)

Review the following "weekly challenge" options, and select the challenge you'd like to do. Turn to a partner, and share your choice. Then make plans to connect with your partner sometime between now and the next session to check in with and encourage one another.

☐ **DO A GOOD DEED.** Find a way to put your faith into action this week. Listen to someone who needs to talk. Love someone who is hurting. Give to someone who is in need. But here's the rub: Don't do it just to do it; do it because of your faith in God...because you *want* to. Faith *wants* to do good works.

☐ **TRUST GOD TO GROW GOOD WORKS FROM YOUR FAITH.** Do you volunteer out of guilt or serve people because you're "supposed to"? Stop! Seriously. God wants you to do those things but with a glad and sincere heart, not a begrudging one. So this week, commit to pray that God would change your heart. If there's something you're "doing for God" that God didn't ask you to do, let it go. Ask God to give you a *desire* to do good works for him and for others.

☐ **THANK SOMEONE FOR HIS OR HER ACTIVE FAITH.** James 2:21-26 describes the obvious results of people who put their faith into action. Do you know someone like this—someone who has truly lived out his or her faith? Write the person a letter (or e-mail), and thank him or her for living out faith and showing God's love to others.

☐ **DO SOME GOOD WORK *TOGETHER*!** As a group, decide on one way you can do good deeds together. Perhaps you can take a cue from this passage and clothe the cold or feed the hungry. Choose a time and place to get together this week and live out your faith.

Come back together as a group. Share prayer requests, and if you're comfortable doing so, share your weekly challenge with the group also. Pray for everyone's needs and that God will give each person in your group opportunities to put his or her faith into action.

Until next time...

Date _____

Time _____

Place _____

Taking It Home:

1. Set a goal for how many times you'll either read through or watch on your DVD the Session 5 Bible passage (James 3:1-18). Make a point to read the "Sense of History" feature in Session 5 (p. 51) before the next session. Let your weekly challenge partner know what goals you've set so he or she can encourage you and help hold you accountable.

2. Touch base sometime before the next session with your weekly challenge partner to compare notes on how you're both doing with the goals you've set.

3. If you have volunteered for a role or signed up to help with food or supplies for the next session, be sure to prepare for this. The Session 5 supplies list can be found on page 48, and the Food Coordinator instructions are on page 104.

4. **I commit to touching my world this week by putting my faith into action in the following ways:**

_____

_____

_____

_____

SESSION 5:

WHAT TASTE DO *YOU* LEAVE?

JAMES 3:1-18

In this session you'll reflect on the importance of controlling your words and be challenged to instead use your words to bring blessing and encouragement.

PRE-SESSION CHECKLIST:

☐ **Leader:** Check out the Session 5 Leader Notes in the back of the book (p. 95).

☐ **Food Coordinator:** If you are responsible for the Session 5 snack, see page 104.

☐ **Supplies:**
  • 1 lighter or pack of matches for each subgroup

TASTE AND SEE (20 minutes)

Take a snack, and settle in. Turn to a partner, and discuss the following:

• What was the biggest challenge you faced today?

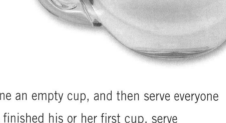

Watch what you say! Seriously, as you converse, think about the words you use to describe people and events.

Gather back together as a large group, and begin your "taste test."

Food Coordinator: Give everyone an empty cup, and then serve everyone from the first pitcher. After everyone has finished his or her first cup, serve everyone from the second pitcher.

After everyone has tried both cups, discuss the following questions:

• How surprised were you by the second cup of water?

• How were the two cups similar? How were they different?

Watch the fifth chapter on the DVD (James 3:1-18).

James 3:1-18

[1]Dear brothers and sisters, not many of you should become teachers in the church, for we who teach will be judged more strictly. [2]Indeed, we all make many mistakes. For if we could control our tongues, we would be perfect and could also control ourselves in every other way.

[3]We can make a large horse go wherever we want by means of a small bit in its mouth. [4]And a small rudder makes a huge ship turn wherever the pilot chooses to go, even though the winds are strong. [5]In the same way, the tongue is a small thing that makes grand speeches.

But a tiny spark can set a great forest on fire. [6]And the tongue is a flame of fire. It is a whole world of wickedness, corrupting your entire body. It can set your whole life on fire, for it is set on fire by hell itself.

[7]People can tame all kinds of animals, birds, reptiles, and fish, [8]but no one can tame the tongue. It is restless and evil, full of deadly poison. [9]Sometimes it praises our Lord and Father, and sometimes it curses those who have been made in the image of God. [10]And so blessing and cursing come pouring out of the same mouth. Surely, my brothers and sisters, this is not right! [11]Does a spring of water bubble out with both fresh water and bitter water? [12]Does a fig tree produce olives, or a grapevine produce figs? No, and you can't draw fresh water from a salty spring.

[13]If you are wise and understand God's ways, prove it by living an honorable life, doing good works with the humility that comes from wisdom. [14]But if you are bitterly jealous and there is selfish ambition in your heart,

don't cover up the truth with boasting and lying. [15]For jealousy and selfishness are not God's kind of wisdom. Such things are earthly, unspiritual, and demonic. [16]For wherever there is jealousy and selfish ambition, there you will find disorder and evil of every kind.

[17]But the wisdom from above is first of all pure. It is also peace loving, gentle at all times, and willing to yield to others. It is full of mercy and good deeds. It shows no favoritism and is always sincere. [18]And those who are peacemakers will plant seeds of peace and reap a harvest of righteousness.

A SENSE OF HISTORY

Which James Wrote the Book of James—and When?

As he didn't specifically identify himself, some debate remains as to *which* James wrote this letter. Many believe the author is Jesus' half-brother James, who became the leader of the church in Jerusalem after Jesus' death and resurrection.

Other suggested authors include the disciple James (the son of Zebedee and brother of disciple John); James the father of the disciple Judas (Thaddaeus, not Iscariot); and the other disciple James (the son of Alphaeus). It has also been suggested that the letter may have been written by someone else and later credited to James.

Knowing *who* wrote this letter also provides clues as to *when* it was written. If Jesus' half-brother James is in fact the author of this letter, it would had to have been written before his death in A.D. 62. It probably also would have been written before the Jerusalem Council of A.D. 49 in which James played such an important role (Acts 15), since there is no mention of it in this letter. The lack of mention of a formal church structure and the use of more "Jewish" terms in this letter also suggest an earlier date.

Therefore, given the evidence, the epistle of James would be one of the earliest finished books of the New Testament, if not *the* earliest.

DIGGING INTO SCRIPTURE (30 minutes)

As a group, discuss:
- What thoughts or emotions came to your mind while watching this session's Bible passage?

Did you know? *The tongue is the strongest muscle in the body. In most cases, it's also the muscle that gets the most exercise.*

Did you also know that the tongue has more than 9,000 taste buds? Bet you wish it had a few thousand less after that second cup of water!

Read James 3:2-12, and answer the following questions:
- How is the tongue described here? How have you seen this to be true in your own words?

- Think about your taste test earlier. Remember the bitter taste you had in your mouth; it may be there even now. In what ways can we leave a bitter taste in the mouths of others by the things we say to them?

Think about it! *Can you imagine growing up as Jesus' little brother? Wonder who Mom and Dad's favorite was? No wonder James was so concerned about his tongue!*

Now break into subgroups.

Leader: Give a lighter or pack of matches to each Subgroup Leader. If you use matches, make sure there's a place to put the burnt ones.

Subgroup Leaders: Agree to come back together in 15 minutes.

As you each take a turn flicking the lighter, or lighting a match, share a brief "fire" story or memory you have.

When everyone has had a chance to "light up," answer the following questions:

• Look at verses 5 and 6 again. Think about the power of a fire, even a small one. What are some things a fire is used for?

> **"**To say, 'You're angry over such a little thing,' is like saying, 'The fire started with just a little match.' It may well be true, but it does nothing to alleviate the present situation.**"**
>
> —Graham Ericsson

• When have you been "burned" by others' words? How did it feel?

• When have you burned others with your words? How did it feel at the time, and how did it feel later on, after you had time to reflect on it?

Come back together as a larger group, and share any highlights or questions from your subgroup discussion.

MAKING IT PERSONAL (15 minutes)

Read James 3:13-18, and answer the following questions:

- What reasons are given in this passage for the negative or hurtful things that come out of our mouths? What others can you think of?

- What alternatives to these kinds of speech does James give us in this passage? What would these changes look like in your own life?

- What other actions or attitudes do you need to change as well so you can replace "bitter water" with "fresh water" in the things you say to others?

Did you know?
Every person has a unique tongue print, just like fingerprints. What prints do you leave behind?

TOUCHING YOUR WORLD (25 minutes)

Review the following "weekly challenge" options, and select the challenge you'd like to do. Turn to a partner, and share your choice. Then make plans to connect with your partner sometime between now and the next session to check in with and encourage one another.

☐ **BE AN ENCOURAGER.** Find someone you can encourage with your words this week. Think carefully about what you'll say to that person, and then commit to seeking out that person so you can say those words that will bring life to him or her.

☐ **MAKE AMENDS.** If there's someone you've hurt with your words—or who has hurt you with his or hers—commit to seeking out him or her and setting things right this week. As you prepare to do so, consider: Do you need help seeing the other side of the argument and/or creative solutions to the problem you're having? Is there a part of the disagreement that you need to own up to and receive forgiveness for as well? Make these points of prayer now and during the week.

☐ **ASK GOD TO HELP YOU LET GO.** Is there a situation in which you've done everything you can to make repairs and/or forgive to the best of your abilities, but you find it coming back to your mind? Commit to praying daily for that situation and that God would reveal any areas that may still need to be dealt with.

☐ **LEARN HOW TO BECOME A PEACEMAKER.** Perhaps your church, your job, or another organization in the area is offering training. Another great resource to make James 3:13-18 a reality in your life—as well as get more formal training on how to be a peacemaker in your church, home, or work environment—is Peacemaker Ministries (www.peacemaker.net).

Come back together as a group. Share prayer requests, and pray for everyone's needs. Be sure to use your tongue to bless others in your group as you pray for them and to speak well of others you're praying for.

Until next time...

Date _____

Time _____

Place _____

Taking It Home:

1. Set a goal for how many times you'll either read through or watch on your DVD the Session 6 Bible passage (James 4:1-12). Make a point to read the "Sense of History" feature in Session 6 (p. 61) before the next session. Let your weekly challenge partner know what goals you've set so he or she can encourage you and help hold you accountable.

2. Touch base sometime before the next session with your weekly challenge partner to compare notes on how you're both doing with the goals you've set.

3. If you have volunteered for a role or signed up to help with food or supplies for the next session, be sure to prepare for this. The Session 6 supplies list can be found on page 58, and the Food Coordinator instructions are on page 104.

4. **I commit to touching my world this week by using my tongue to show Jesus' love in the following ways:**

_____

_____

_____

_____

SESSION 6:

CHOOSING YOUR DESIRES WISELY

JAMES 4:1-12

In this session you'll reflect on how to make God your first priority and how your life will be changed as you do so.

PRE-SESSION CHECKLIST:

☐ **Leader:** Check out the Session 6 Leader Notes in the back of the book (p. 96).

☐ **Food Coordinator:** If you are responsible for the Session 6 snack, see page 104.

☐ **Supplies:**

- several work-related items—include an item of work clothing, laptop computer, tool
- 1 family photo album or framed family photo
- objects representing hobbies or personal interests—football, muffin tin, musical instrument, pillow
    - 1 normal-size Bible
    - 1 small suitcase
    - 1 colored marker for each person in the group
    - one 3x5-inch blank sticker or label for each person in the group

58

TASTE AND SEE (20 minutes)

Today's snack is trail mix—great food for when you're traveling. Enjoy it, and as you eat, discuss the following questions:

- What's the farthest you've ever been from home?

- If you could take a vacation anywhere in the world, where would you go? Why?

- Imagine you were taking a long trip out of the country. If you could pack only three things in your suitcase, what would you take?

Watch the sixth chapter on the DVD (James 4:1-12).

James 4:1-12

[1]What is causing the quarrels and fights among you? Don't they come from the evil desires at war within you? [2]You want what you don't have, so you scheme and kill to get it. You are jealous of what others have, but you can't get it, so you fight and wage war to take it away from them. Yet you don't have what you want because you don't ask God for it. [3]And even when you ask, you don't get it because your motives are all wrong—you want only what will give you pleasure.

[4]You adulterers! Don't you realize that friendship with the world makes you an enemy of God? I say it again: If you want to be a friend of the world, you make yourself an enemy of God. [5]What do you think the Scriptures mean when they say that the spirit God has placed within us is filled with envy? [6]But he gives us even more grace to stand against such evil desires. As the Scriptures say,

"God opposes the proud
but favors the humble."

[7]So humble yourselves before God. Resist the devil, and he will flee from you. [8]Come close to God, and God will come close to you. Wash your hands, you sinners; purify your hearts, for your loyalty is divided between God and the world. [9]Let there be tears for what you have done. Let there be sorrow and deep grief. Let there be sadness

instead of laughter, and gloom instead of joy. [10]Humble yourselves before the Lord, and he will lift you up in honor.

[11]Don't speak evil against each other, dear brothers and sisters. If you criticize and judge each other, then you are criticizing and judging God's law. But your job is to obey the law, not to judge whether it applies to you. [12]God alone, who gave the law, is the Judge. He alone has the power to save or to destroy. So what right do you have to judge your neighbor?

A SENSE OF HISTORY
Choosing to Stand for Jesus

James wanted nothing to do with a world that despised his Lord and Savior. He flat-out rejected the prideful, self-centered beliefs of many of the people of his day and ultimately paid the price for it. James suffered the toughest kind of humility when the high priest and other Jewish religious leaders in Jerusalem had him stoned to death in A.D. 62.

His execution was widely regarded in the Jewish community as unfair; in fact, Josephus' account of his death called it "little more than judicial murder" and reported that most people in the area were so upset about James' death that they deposed the high priest responsible for it.

James probably could have fought the execution order in the courts and won. But he wanted only God to be exalted, and he demonstrated his genuine humility by accepting his death sentence. It was this kind of deep commitment, even in death, that caused the Apostle Paul to call James one of the three "pillars" of the church (Galatians 2:9).

DIGGING INTO SCRIPTURE (30 minutes)

As a group, discuss:

• What thoughts or emotions came to your mind while watching this session's Bible passage?

Now break into subgroups.

Subgroup Leaders: Plan to come back together in 15 minutes.

Read James 4:1-5, and answer the following questions:

• Think about the trail mix you ate. It was a good mix of different ingredients. But sometimes *people* don't mix so easily; they get angry at each other over worldly things and lose sight of Jesus' love. What are some examples of the kinds of things that divide people?

• In what ways do material possessions draw you away from God?

• Where do you draw the line between "friendship with the world" and being an "enemy of God"? Why there?

Come back together as a larger group, and share your answers with one another.

Leader: Bring out the suitcase, and place it open in front of the group. Also bring out the work-related items, family photo album, objects representing personal interests, and Bible; and place them near the suitcase but not in it.

One at a time, each person should pick up one of the items—whether it's related to work, family, hobby, or your relationship with God. Share a few words about what this item represents in your life, and place it in the suitcase.

Leader: After everyone has taken a turn, try to shut the suitcase.

Answer the following questions:

• When you're traveling, you make room in your suitcase for the most important things. What do you consider to be the most important things in your life?

• Think about a time you were under a lot of pressure. What were the first things in your "suitcase" to go? Why did you choose those things?

• What has distracted you from a genuine friendship with God, either now or in the past? What changes did you, or can you, make so that God is given priority?

> **Did you know?**
> The Apostle James didn't need a suitcase. While Paul and other early Christian leaders traveled quite a bit, it's believed that James never left Jerusalem.

As a larger group, read James 4:6-12.

Leader: Give everyone a 3x5-inch sticker or label and a colored marker.

Write (or draw) on your sticker one thing you can choose to do to show humility—whether it's submitting an area of your life to God, forgiving someone (or asking his or her forgiveness), offering to clean someone's home, or some other act of humility.

Place the labels on the outside of the suitcase, which should still be in the middle of the floor. Since the suitcase represents your life and the things you carry around with you, it now will also represent what a humble life looks like as other people see it.

When everyone has finished, answer the following questions:

• Look at verse 8 again. When have you felt "divided between God and the world"? What choice did you finally make? What was the result?

• When has humbling yourself helped you experience closeness with God? closeness with others?

• Think about the sticker you placed on the suitcase. What can you do this week to make the choice represented on that sticker a reality?

TOUCHING YOUR WORLD (25 minutes)

Review the following "weekly challenge" options, and select the challenge you'd like to do. Turn to a partner, and share your choice. Then make plans to connect with your partner sometime between now and the next session to check in with and encourage one another.

☐ **BE THE NON-CENTER OF ATTENTION.** Resolve that when you encounter a situation in which you are typically the focus of attention, you'll give someone else the limelight by giving him or her credit or praise for a job well done. Likewise, the next time someone compliments you, choose to simply thank that person for his or her kind words. Don't discount the encouragement by downplaying your abilities. It's an act of humility to *accept* praise from another person, too.

☐ **BOX UP AN EARTHLY TREASURE.** Find something in your home to which you've given too much of your attention and desire. Wrap it up in a box, and place it in your basement or attic for at least a week. Then think about how much priority that item really should have in your life. Consider giving that item away, if it makes sense to do so.

☐ **GET YOUR HANDS DIRTY.** Follow Jesus' humble example of washing his disciples' feet by doing a modern-day act of service for a friend. Scrub a bathroom, sweep a garage, or dust the nooks and crannies. Take on the kind of job many people avoid when they can.

Come back together as a group. Share prayer requests, and then pray for everyone's needs. Take this time to pray about the choices you've made today and how God may want to use you this week.

Until next time...

Date _____

Time _____

Place _____

Taking It Home:

1. Set a goal for how many times you'll either read through or watch on your DVD the Session 7 Bible passage (James 4:13–5:6). Make a point to read the "Sense of History" feature in Session 7 (p. 71) before the next session. Let your weekly challenge partner know what goals you've set so he or she can encourage you and help hold you accountable.

2. Touch base sometime before the next session with your weekly challenge partner to compare notes on how you're both doing with the goals you've set.

3. If you have volunteered for a role or signed up to help with food or supplies for the next session, be sure to prepare for this. The Session 7 supplies list can be found on page 68, and the Food Coordinator instructions are on page 105.

4. **I commit to touching my world this week by making the following choices for Jesus:**

_____

_____

_____

_____

SESSION 7:

THE WAGES OF WEALTH

JAMES 4:13–5:6

In this session you'll explore the problems wealth can bring to your relationship with Jesus and how to avoid them.

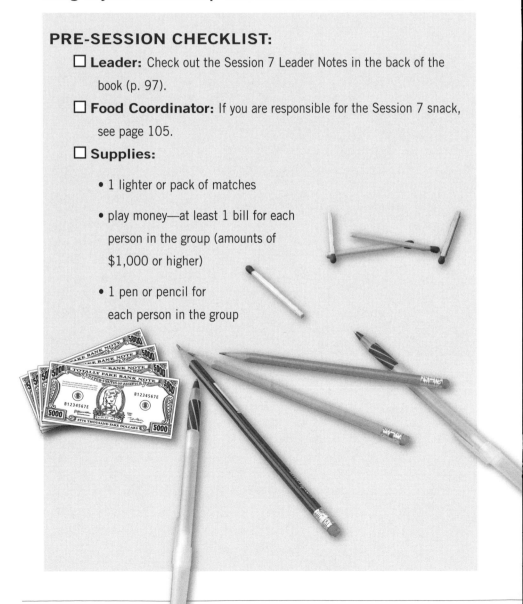

PRE-SESSION CHECKLIST:

☐ **Leader:** Check out the Session 7 Leader Notes in the back of the book (p. 97).

☐ **Food Coordinator:** If you are responsible for the Session 7 snack, see page 105.

☐ **Supplies:**

- 1 lighter or pack of matches

- play money—at least 1 bill for each person in the group (amounts of $1,000 or higher)

- 1 pen or pencil for each person in the group

TASTE AND SEE (20 minutes)

For this session, your snack is mint ice cream. Enjoy!

While enjoying the snack, find a partner, and discuss the following questions:

• What plans do you have for the upcoming weekend?

• Do you have any vacation plans in your future? If so, what are they?

Gather back together as a large group, and share some of your answers. Then discuss:

• What's your favorite ice cream flavor?

• If you could eat all the ice cream you wanted (without gaining weight, clogging your arteries, or straining your budget), would you? Why or why not?

 Watch the seventh chapter on the DVD (James 4:13–5:6).

James 4:13–5:6

¹³Look here, you who say, "Today or tomorrow we are going to a certain town and will stay there a year. We will do business there and make a profit." ¹⁴How do you know what your life will be like tomorrow? Your life is like the morning fog—it's here a little while, then it's gone. ¹⁵What you ought to say is, "If the Lord wants us to, we will live and do this or that." ¹⁶Otherwise you are boasting about your own plans, and all such boasting is evil.

¹⁷Remember, it is sin to know what you ought to do and then not do it.

^{5:1}Look here, you rich people: Weep and groan with anguish because of all the terrible troubles ahead of you. ²Your wealth is rotting away, and your fine clothes are moth-eaten rags. ³Your gold and silver have become worthless. The very wealth you were counting on will eat away your flesh like fire. This treasure you have accumulated will stand as evidence against you on the day of judgment. ⁴For listen! Hear the cries of the field workers whom you have cheated of their pay. The wages you held back cry out against you. The cries of those who harvest your fields have reached the ears of the Lord of Heaven's Armies.

⁵You have spent your years on earth in luxury, satisfying your every desire. You have fattened yourselves for the day of slaughter. ⁶You have condemned and killed innocent people, who do not resist you.

A SENSE OF HISTORY
Poor James

Although the Apostle James was the head of the Christian church in Jerusalem, he chose to live an ascetic life. He kept things simple—his clothes, food, and home were not only modest but probably bordered on poverty-level standards. Some traditional accounts of James say he wore nothing but thin rags, never cut his hair, and never even bathed. He denied himself just about every possible earthly desire—and likely some needs as well. Nothing would stand in the way of his committed, live-it-like-you-mean-it brand of faith.

James may have learned much of his lessons on wealth from his brother, Jesus Christ. Jesus said in Matthew 8:20, "Foxes have dens to live in, and birds have nests, but the Son of Man has no place even to lay his head." James' letter draws heavily from Jesus' Sermon on the Mount, in which Jesus spoke repeatedly about money, possessions, and humility.

James doesn't say riches themselves are bad, but he severely warns that wealth is temporary and, worse yet, can ultimately destroy your life. "James the Just" not only believed his life on Earth was a vapor but fully exemplified it through his lifestyle. To James, how you used your life and wealth was a visible sign of an invisible faith.

DIGGING INTO SCRIPTURE (30 minutes)

As a group, discuss:

• What thoughts or emotions came to your mind while watching this session's Bible passage?

Now break into subgroups.

Subgroup Leaders: Give yourselves 15 minutes for your discussion time.

Read James 4:13–5:6, and answer the following questions:

• Why do you think James is so concerned about how his fellow Christians approach their futures?

> *Did you know? An estimated 640 million children in our world lack adequate shelter, 400 million don't have access to safe water, 270 million have no access to health care, and 90 million experience some degree of starvation. (UNICEF State of the World's Children report, 2005)*

• Think about the ice cream you ate earlier. If money is like ice cream, why are so many people consumed by the pursuit of wealth?

• Can you think of a time you didn't have enough money for what you wanted but were able to get by without it? If so, how would your life be different now if you'd received what you thought you needed?

Come back together as a larger group, and share your answers with one another.

 Leader: Give everyone in the group a bill of play money.

Let's say this is real money that you could walk out of here right now and spend. Answer the following questions:

• If you could spend this money on yourself as a gift, what would you buy?

- How would your life be different a year from now if you were actually able to buy that gift for yourself?

> **"***This amazed them. But Jesus said again, 'Dear children, it is very hard to enter the Kingdom of God. In fact, it is easier for a camel to go through the eye of a needle than for a rich person to enter the Kingdom of God!'***"**
> —Mark 10:24-25

- How might your life (or someone else's life) be different one year from now if you asked *God* how you should use the money?

- In this passage, James says wealth can lead to pride, injustice, and selfishness. Is there a way to gain some amount of wealth and still avoid those sins? Explain.

MAKING IT PERSONAL (15 minutes)

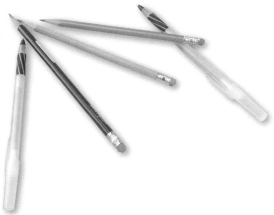

Still have your paper money? Good. Turn it over, and on the back of your bill, write down something in your life that you've been giving more priority than your friendship with God. Maybe it's a material possession, a savings account, or a plan for the future.

Leader: Bring back your ice-cream container, and place it in the middle of the group.

When everyone has finished writing, take out your lighter and your paper money. One person at a time, burn your bill above the container of leftover, melted ice cream. Let the ashes fall into the container.

When everyone has finished, answer the following questions:

- If wealth is truly temporary, what should be your attitude toward it? How can you maintain that attitude?

- How can you be sure that you are truly approaching your plans, money, and possessions in humility and submission to God?

- What checks can you put in place to keep yourself accountable to God and others regarding your plans and possessions?

> ### *Think about it!*
> What Francis Bacon said about 400 years ago still rings true today: "Money is like muck, not good except it be spread."

TOUCHING YOUR WORLD (25 minutes)

Review the following "weekly challenge" options, and select the challenge you'd like to do. Turn to a partner, and share your choice. Then make plans to connect with your partner sometime between now and the next session to check in with and encourage one another.

☐ **JOURNAL YOUR SPENDING HABITS.** For the next seven days, write down everything you spend your money on. At the end of the week, add up how much you spent on yourself, how much on necessities, and how much to bless God or other people. If God reveals a need to change your spending habits, resolve to make that change.

☐ **GO ON A "SPENDING FAST."** For a week, buy absolutely nothing that you don't truly need (such as gas for your car so you can get to work or milk for your kids to eat their cereal). See for yourself how much your life is affected by leaving out unnecessary purchases.

☐ **GIVE YOUR STUFF TO CHARITY.** Gather items from your home that you know you can do without. Then donate all those things to a local charitable organization. Or have a garage sale and donate your earnings to a favorite ministry or charity.

☐ **SPEND YOUR "SPENDING MONEY" ON SOMEONE ELSE.** If you set aside a certain amount of spending money for yourself for the week (such as for buying a coffee every day or purchasing a new article of clothing), set aside that money instead for someone who really needs it, and use it on him or her. That person will be blessed that you did.

Come back together as a group. Share prayer requests.

Food Coordinator: Give a mint breath strip to everyone in the group.

Think once more about the ice cream you shared at the beginning of the session. Now think of the mint breath strip as a reminder of the temporary nature of the things we have as well as the freshness of submitting our lives and our wealth to God. Put the breath strip in your mouth, and say a brief word of thanks to God for providing for your needs. Then pray together for everyone's needs.

Until next time...

Date _____

Time _____

Place _____

Taking It Home:

1. Set a goal for how many times you'll either read through or watch on your DVD the Session 8 Bible passage (James 5:7-20). Also read the "Sense of History" feature in Session 8 (p. 81) before the next session. If you haven't yet, now would be a good time to watch the entire book of James in one sitting. (It takes about 16 minutes.) Let your weekly challenge partner know what goals you've set so he or she can encourage you and help hold you accountable.

2. Touch base sometime before the next session with your weekly challenge partner to compare notes on how you're both doing with the goals you've set.

3. If you have volunteered for a role or signed up to help with food or supplies for the next session, be sure to prepare for this. The Session 8 supplies list can be found on page 78, and the Food Coordinator instructions are on page 105.

4. **I commit to touching my world this week by trusting my wealth to God in the following ways:** _____

_____

SESSION 8:

PRESSING FORWARD IN PRAYER

JAMES 5:7-20

In this session you'll focus on the power of prayer and patiently trusting God.

PRE-SESSION CHECKLIST:

☐ **Leader:** Check out the Session 8 Leader Notes in the back of the book (p. 98).

☐ **Food Coordinator:** If you are responsible for the Session 8 snack, see page 105.

☐ **Supplies:**

- at least 3 sheets of paper per person
- 1 marker for each person
- masking tape (or other means of safely attaching papers to the wall)

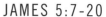

TASTE AND SEE (20 minutes)

After today's food has finally been served, discuss the following questions:

- What was it like having to wait for this session's snack?

- What other "little things" often test your patience?

- On the other hand, what are some little things you've come to appreciate about this group as you've worked through this study of James?

Watch the final chapter on the DVD (James 5:7-20).

James 5:7-20

[7]Dear brothers and sisters, be patient as you wait for the Lord's return. Consider the farmers who patiently wait for the rains in the fall and in the spring. They eagerly look for the valuable harvest to ripen. [8]You, too, must be patient. Take courage, for the coming of the Lord is near.

[9]Don't grumble about each other, brothers and sisters, or you will be judged. For look—the Judge is standing at the door!

[10]For examples of patience in suffering, dear brothers and sisters, look at the prophets who spoke in the name of the Lord. [11]We give great honor to those who endure under suffering. For instance, you know about Job, a man of great endurance. You can see how the Lord was kind to him at the end, for the Lord is full of tenderness and mercy.

[12]But most of all, my brothers and sisters, never take an oath, by heaven or earth or anything else. Just say a simple yes or no, so that you will not sin and be condemned.

[13]Are any of you suffering hardships? You should pray. Are any of you happy? You should sing praises. [14]Are any of you sick? You should call for the elders of the church to come and pray over you, anointing you with oil in the name of the Lord. [15]Such a prayer offered in faith will heal the sick, and the Lord will make you well. And if you have committed any sins, you will be forgiven.

[16]Confess your sins to each other and pray for each other so that you may be healed. The earnest prayer of a righteous person has great

80

power and produces wonderful results. [17]Elijah was as human as we are, and yet when he prayed earnestly that no rain would fall, none fell for three and a half years! [18]Then, when he prayed again, the sky sent down rain, and the earth began to yield its crops.

[19]My dear brothers and sisters, if someone among you wanders away from the truth and is brought back, [20]you can be sure that whoever brings the sinner back will save that person from death and bring about the forgiveness of many sins.

A SENSE OF HISTORY

Great Expectations!

The book of Acts opens with Jesus' ascension into heaven and the promise that "someday he will return from heaven in the same way you saw him go!" (Acts 1:11). At this time in the history of the church (10 to 20 years after Jesus' death and resurrection), most Christians believed that Jesus would return to Earth in their lifetimes.

The expectation was so great that sometime after James' letter, the Apostle Paul had to assure the Thessalonian church that those who had died before Jesus' return still belonged to Jesus: "We want you to know what will happen to the believers who have died so you will not grieve like people who have no hope. For since we believe that Jesus died and was raised to life again, we also believe that when Jesus returns, God will bring back with him all the believers who have died" (1 Thessalonians 4:13-14).

The people to whom James was writing were also crying out to God for help in their suffering. Thus, it was a comfort to be reminded to be patient until the Lord's return. They were hoping—as many Christians do today—that Jesus would come, free them from their suffering, and take them to live with him in heaven.

DIGGING INTO SCRIPTURE (30 minutes)

As a group, discuss:

• What thoughts or emotions came to your mind while watching this session's Bible passage?

• What have your overall impressions been as you've interacted with the book of James? How has God spoken to you through this study?

Now break into subgroups.

> **On your own time:**
> *James wanted suffering Christians everywhere to remember the story of Job, a man who trusted God despite awful circumstances (James 5:11). You can read the whole story in the book of Job.*

Subgroup Leaders: Take no more than 15 minutes for your discussion time.

Read James 5:7-12 together, and then answer the following questions:

• How was waiting for tonight's snack similar to the ways you wait for God to answer your prayers? How was it different?

• How hard is it for you to be patient and trust God? Be honest.

- How does having that kind of patience and trust (or lack of it) affect your life? the lives around you?

- Look again at verse 8. How does knowing "the coming of the Lord is near" help you have patience? What other ways of looking forward help you be patient in tough times?

Come back together as a larger group, and share any highlights or questions from your subgroup discussion.

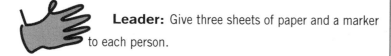 **Leader:** Give three sheets of paper and a marker to each person.

Think of times you know prayer has made a difference in the outcome. Write down at least two or three experiences on separate sheets of paper, large enough to be read from several feet away. Write down personal examples, examples you've heard of from other people, or biblical examples.

Leader: Give group members five minutes to write. Then give a piece of masking tape to everyone, and show group members where to post their answered prayers.

> "Don't worry about anything; instead, pray about everything. Tell God what you need, and thank him for all he has done. Then you will experience God's peace, which exceeds anything we can understand. His peace will guard your hearts and minds as you live in Christ Jesus."
> —Philippians 4:6-7

Tape up all your sheets in the area the Leader has designated. As a group, take a few minutes to read all the examples of answered prayer. After everyone has had a chance to absorb these examples, read James 5:13-18, and answer the following questions:

• Think about a time of personal (spiritual/emotional) drought in your own life. What was it like? What changed to end that drought?

• How did looking at all these answered prayers impact your own feelings on prayer?

On your own time:
James gives another biblical example in verses 17-18: Elijah announcing, in response to the evil of the people of Israel and in obedience to God, that it would not rain again until he said it would. Three years later, Elijah prayed, and a downpour refreshed the land. Read the whole story, in 1 Kings 17–18.

• How would your life be different if you depended more on God in prayer? What changes do you need to make so this is possible?

MAKING IT PERSONAL (15 minutes)

Read James 5:19-20 together, and answer the following questions:

- How does this passage relate to this session's teaching on patience?

- What prayer or prayers have you been praying for a long time? For a loved one to make a faith commitment (or to recommit his or her life) to Jesus? For healing? For something else? Have you ever been tempted to give up? What keeps you going?

- What can you draw from this passage and the examples you've seen during this session to help you continue to persevere in prayer?

> **Did you know?**
> Church tradition says James was known as "Old Camel Knees" because he spent so much time in prayer that his knees became hard and calloused as a camel's.

TOUCHING YOUR WORLD (*??* minutes)

Review the following "weekly challenge" options, and then select the challenge you'd like to do. Turn to a partner, and share your choice. Then make plans to connect with your partner in the next week to check in with and encourage one another.

☐ **CREATE AND MAINTAIN A PRAYER LIST.** Make a list of people or things you want to pray regularly for. Include praises as well as concerns. Include world and community needs as well as your own. Include family members and friends as well as casual contacts who may need a special touch from God. Then pray through your list—regularly. Keep track of answered prayers, and keep adding new concerns to the list. It will be rewarding to look back and see all the prayers God has answered.

☐ **CONFESS YOUR SINS.** If you feel there is some kind of habitual or other sin coming between you and the Lord, confess it to God. Consider confessing it to a trusted Christian friend or leader as well (see James 5:16). Ask that person to pray for you, extend Christ-like forgiveness to you, and perhaps also continue to pray with you and keep you accountable in that area.

☐ **CLUSTER WITH A FEW OTHERS TO PRAY.** Call a few friends, and have them join you for a prayer time this week. It could be at someone's home, at the church, or in any quiet spot where you can gather. Pray for needs within your group and any other needs you know of. Your entire group could do this option, if you choose.

Come back together as a group.

Prayer Coordinator: Give out the prayer lists you've prepared.

Put what you've just studied into action right now. Share prayer concerns with one another, use the prayer list, and pray for everyone's needs as long as you have time. Make this not just a time of prayer but also a time to *really* trust God in prayer for those concerns.

Take time also to thank God specifically for things he has done in your group's lives during this study.

Leader: If you haven't already, take some time to discuss what's next for the group. Will you stay together and work on another *BibleSense* book? Will you celebrate your time together with a party and be done? Or will you have a party and *then* start another *BibleSense* book the following week?

Touch-base time:

Set a date, time, and place to get together with your weekly challenge partner in the next week.

Date _____

Time _____

Place _____

Taking It Home:

1. Touch base during the week with your weekly challenge partner to compare notes on how you're both doing with the goals you've set.

2. You may want to review this week's passage or even watch the entire book of James straight through on your DVD now that you've finished your study.

3. **I commit to touching my world this week by regularly and prayerfully entrusting the following to God:**

_____

_____

NOTES & ROLES

CONTENTS

LEADER NOTES

GROUP ROLES

LEADER NOTES

GENERAL LEADER TIPS

1. Although these sessions are designed to require minimum advance preparation, try to read over each session ahead of time and watch the DVD chapter for that session. Highlight any questions you feel are especially important for your group to spend time on during the session.

2. Prior to the first session, watch the "Leading a *BibleSense* Session" overview on the DVD. You'll notice that this isn't your average Bible study. Food? Activities? Don't forget that Jesus used food and everyday items and experiences in *his* small group all the time. Jesus' disciples certainly weren't comfortable when he washed their feet (John 13:5-17) and were even a bit confused at first. Jesus reassured them, "You don't understand now what I am doing, but someday you will" (verse 7), and it turned out to be a powerful lesson that stayed with them for the rest of their lives. It's our prayer that your group will have similar experiences.

3. Take the time to read the group roles on pages 100-102, and make sure all critical tasks and roles are covered for each session. The three roles you *absolutely need filled* for each session are Leader, Host, and Food Coordinator. These roles can be rotated around the group if you like.

4. Discuss as a group how to handle child care—not only because it can be a sensitive subject but also to give your group an opportunity to begin working together as a group. See the Child Care Coordinator tips on page 111 for ideas on how to handle this important issue.

5. Don't be afraid to ask for volunteers. Who knows—they may want to commit to a role once they've tried it (and if it's available on a regular basis). However, give people the option of "no thanks" as well.

6. Every session will begin with a snack, so work closely with your Food Coordinator—he or she has a vital role in each session. If you need to, go ahead and ask for donations from your group for the snacks that are provided each week.

7. Always start on time. If you do this from Session 1, you'll avoid the group arriving and starting later as the study goes on.

8. Be ready and willing to pray at times other than the closing time. Start each session with prayer, and let group members know they're getting down to business. Be open to other times prayer is appropriate, such as when someone answers a question and ends up expressing pain or grief over a situation he or she is currently struggling with. Don't save it for the end; stop and pray right there and then. Your Prayer Coordinator can take the lead in these situations if you like, but give him or her permission to do so.

9. Try not to have the first or last word on every question (or even most of them). Give everyone the opportunity to participate. At the same time, don't put anyone on the spot. Remind group members that they can pass on any questions they're not comfortable answering.

10. Keep things on track. There are suggested time limits for each section. Encourage good discussion, but don't be afraid to rope 'em back in. If you do decide to spend extra time on a question or activity, consider skipping or spending less time on a later question or activity so you can stay on schedule.

11. Don't let your group off the hook with the assignments in the "Touching Your World" section. This is when group members get to apply in a personal way what they have learned. Encourage group members to follow through on their assignments. You may even want to make it a point to ask how they did with their weekly challenges during snack time at the beginning of your next session.

12. Also note that the last weekly challenge in "Touching Your World" is often an outreach assignment that can be done either individually or as a group. Make sure group members who take on these challenges are encouraged and, if it's a group activity, organized. If your group has an Outreach Coordinator, let him or her take the lead here, and touch base regularly.

13. Last, the single most important thing a leader can do for his or her group is spend time in prayer for group members. Why not take a minute to pray for your group right now?

Session 1 Leader Notes

1. Read the General Leader Tips, starting on page 89, if you haven't already. Take a peek at the tips for other group roles as well (pp. 103-111).

2. Make sure everyone has a *BibleSense* book and DVD. Have group members pass around their books to record contact information (p. 7) before or during "Taste and See" or at the end of the session.

3. If this is the first time you're meeting as a group, you may want to take a few minutes before your session to lay down some ground rules. Here are three simple ones:

- Don't say anything that will embarrass anyone or violate someone's trust.

- Likewise, anything shared in the group stays in the group, unless the person sharing it says otherwise.

- No one has to answer a question he or she is uncomfortable answering.

4. Take time to review the group roles on pages 100-102 before you get together, and be ready to discuss them at the end of your session. Assign as many roles as you can, but don't pressure anyone to take on something he or she doesn't want or isn't yet sure about.

5. For this session, you're responsible for the items in the supplies list on page 8. You'll want to assign the supplies list for future sessions; the Host is the most sensible choice to handle this responsibility, or it can be rotated around the group.

6. Note the item in the supplies list and its use in "Digging Into Scripture." Ideally, you'll want a pair of binoculars for every member of the group. Recruit other group members to bring pairs. If binoculars are difficult to locate, you could substitute telescopes or even microscopes. The idea is to give group members a different perspective. That said, binoculars are probably easier to find (and easier to share!).

7. Unless you're ahead of the game and already have a Food Coordinator, you're responsible for the snack for this first session. You'll want to make sure you have a Food Coordinator for future sessions, but for this session, be sure to review the Food Coordinator assignment on page 103.

8. Before you dismiss this first session, make a special point to remind group members of the importance of following through on the weekly challenge each of them has committed to in the "Touching Your World" section.

Session 2 Leader Notes

1. If new people join the group this session, use part of the "Taste and See" time to ask them to introduce themselves to the group, and have the group members pass around their books to record contact information (p. 7). Give a brief summary of the points covered in Session 1.

2. If you told the group during the first session that you'd be following up to see how they did with their "Touching Your World" commitments, be sure to do so. This is an opportunity to establish an environment of accountability. However, be prepared to share how you did with your *own* commitment from the first session.

3. This week's snack is an activity as well. Your group will be "making faces"—their own—with items supplied by the Food Coordinator. Be sure butter knives are available for group members to do this activity. Note also the "Extra Impact" activity in the margin, and decide whether you'll do this as a group.

4. For this session, you'll need to make a few areas with wall mirrors available—bathrooms, bedrooms, anywhere with a mirror. You'll need enough to accommodate as many subgroups as you have. Talk to your Host about this beforehand. Also, we'll say it one more time here: Use *dry-erase* markers on your mirrors for this activity; they wipe off very easily. And make sure you know your dry-erase markers from your fine-point markers (which are also on the supplies list for this session).

5. For the closing prayer time, ask for volunteers to pray for requests that were shared. You may want to ask the Prayer Coordinator, if you have one, in advance to lead the prayer time. If you don't have a Prayer Coordinator, look over the Prayer Coordinator tips on page 109, and keep them in mind if you lead your prayer time. If you ask someone else to lead, try to ask him or her, and direct him or her to these tips, in advance. Also, if your group has decided to use a prayer list, make sure you use it during your prayer time.

Session 3 Leader Notes

1. See the supplies list and the sensory experience in "Digging Into Scripture." There's one more item not on the supplies list that you'll need: Collect a variety of pictures of people, one picture for each envelope. Include a selection of famous and/or notorious people everyone would recognize (such as politicians, entertainers, or sports figures) as well as a few people from other levels of society (middle-class, poor, even homeless) and perhaps a few of different races or religions. The idea is to evoke a variety of reactions so group members will consider their reactions and how they stack up against God's love for all of us, regardless of who or what we are.

2. If your group chooses the "Reach out as a group" option in "Touching Your World," use part of your prayer time to pray for what situation you want to minister to as a group and what God would want each group member's role in that to be. For example, one person might be assigned the task of identifying specific needs in your community and assessing how to come alongside as a small group; another might be responsible for materials or transportation. Be specific in your planning.

3. Are you praying for your group members regularly? It's the most important thing a leader can do for his or her group. Take some time now to pray for your group if you haven't already.

Session 4 Leader Notes

1. Congratulations! You're halfway through this study. It's time for a checkup: How's the group going? What's worked well so far? What might you consider changing as you approach the remaining sessions?

2. On that note, you may find it helpful to make some notes right after your session to help you evaluate how things are going. Ask yourself, "Did everyone participate?" and "Is there anyone I need to make a special effort to follow up with before the next session?"

3. Note the supplies list and the sensory experience in "Making It Personal." Six-inch pots are recommended, but you can use another size if you like, as long as both pots are the same size. Carefully consider which potted plant you want to use because after the first question in "Making It Personal," you will cut off small pieces of that plant to give to group members to take home.

Also, for the closing part of this experience, it's not necessary to fill the water cups to the top—you don't want to drown the seed or make a mess. You may want to put a towel under the pot with the seed in it, just in case.

4. If group members have chosen to "Do some good work *together*!" in "Touching Your World," use part of your prayer time to pray for that situation and what God would want you to do together.

Session 5 Leader Notes

1. Remember the importance of starting and ending on time, and remind your group of it, too, if you need to.

2. This also would be a good time to remind group members of the importance of following through on the weekly challenge each of them has committed to in "Touching Your World."

Session 6 Leader Notes

1. See the supplies list as well as the sensory experience in "Digging Into Scripture." Include some large or bulky items so that closing the suitcase will be difficult, if not impossible. **Extra Impact:** Challenge people on the spot to give up something they currently have on them—wallet, pocketbook, or some other item. (Of course they can have it back after your session!)

Leave the suitcase in the room for the rest of this session. Also, note that the stickers/labels will be placed *on* the suitcase, so make sure you use a suitcase you're OK with doing that to.

2. How are you doing with your prayer time for the group? Take some time to pray for your group now if you haven't done so already.

Session 7 Leader Notes

1. Since your next session will be your group's last one in this book, you may want to start discussing with the group what to do after you've completed this study.

2. On that note, you may want to do another group checkup before you begin your next study (if that's the plan). Ask yourself, "Is everyone participating?" and "Is there anyone I need to make a special effort to follow up with?"

3. See the supplies list as well as the sensory experience in "Digging Into Scripture." Again, make sure they're "big bills"—$1,000 or higher. The higher they are, the more interesting the responses will probably get. By the way, don't expect to be able to reuse your play money after this session!

4. Also, make sure you keep the ice-cream container from your "Taste and See" time, whether it's empty or there's still some melted ice cream in it. You'll need it for later in the session. Read through the "Making It Personal" activity to see why. You may want to put a tray underneath your container when you bring it out during this time to make sure nothing in the house gets stained.

Session 8 Leader Notes

1. Since this is your group's last session in this book, make sure you have a plan for next week...and beyond.

2. As part of this last session, you may want to consider having people share, either during the "Taste and See" section or at the end of your session, what this study or group has meant to them. This can also be incorporated into the beginning of your prayer time if you like.

3. Take special note of your Food Coordinator's assignment for this session, on page 105. Work together with your Food Coordinator and Host to make sure the delay in serving this snack goes according to plan.

4. Also take note of the supplies list and the sensory experience in "Digging Into Scripture" where the items will be used. Before you meet, discuss with your Host where, and by what means, group members will post their answered prayers so the whole group will see them.

5. Because of this session's focus, your group will spend more time than usual in prayer today. In addition to your regular prayer list, prepare a list of prayer concerns related to your church and community. Give out the list during your prayer time at the end of this session. Give this responsibility to your Prayer Coordinator, if your group has one.

6. Here's another suggestion for making the closing prayer time for this last session special: Have the group form a prayer circle. Then have each person or couple, if comfortable doing so, take a turn standing or kneeling in the middle of the circle while the group prays specifically for them. Your Prayer Coordinator is a good candidate to lead this.

7. Another prayer suggestion: Have group members open and extend their hands as they pray and literally "hand" their concerns over to God. Then have them draw their hands back in as they "receive" back from God in prayer.

8. Also, if someone in your group is willing and able, consider literally putting James 5:14-15 into practice. Ask an elder or person leading this part of the prayer time to bring oil for anointing, and have an extended time of prayer for those in your group who have been struggling with sickness.

9. If you choose, as a group, to do the "Cluster with a few others to pray" option in "Touching Your World," take time at the end of your session to plan a date, time, and place to get together.

GROUP ROLES

ROLE DESCRIPTIONS

Review the group roles that follow.

We have provided multiple roles to encourage maximum participation. At minimum, there are three roles that we recommend be filled for every session—Leader, Food Coordinator, and Host. These particular roles can also be rotated around the group if you like. Other roles (Outreach and Inreach Coordinators especially) are best handled by one person, as they involve tasks that may take more than one week to accomplish. It's *your* group—you decide what works best. What's most important is that you work together in deciding.

Not everyone will want to take on a role, so no pressure. But as you come to own a role in your group, you'll feel more connected. You'll even become more comfortable with that role you're not so sure you want to volunteer for right now.

Read through the following roles together, and write in your book each volunteer's name after his or her role so everyone remembers who's who (and what roles may still be available).

LEADER _____.

Your session Leader will facilitate each session, keeping discussions and activities on track. If a role hasn't yet been filled or the person who normally has a certain role misses a session, the session Leader will also make sure that all tasks and supplies are covered.

FOOD COORDINATOR _____.

The Food Coordinator will oversee the snacks for each group meeting. This role not only builds the fellowship of the group but is an especially important role for this particular study, since specific snacks are assigned for each session and are used to lead group members into the meaning of each session.

HOST _____.

Your Host will open up his or her home and help group members and visitors feel *at* home. It sounds simple enough, but the gift of hospitality is critical to your group. If group members don't feel welcome, chances are they won't stay group members for long. Your Host should also be responsible for supplying, or locating someone who *can* supply, the items in the supplies list at the beginning of each session. (They're usually common household items, so don't panic.)

OUTREACH COORDINATOR _____.

Different sessions often highlight different ways to reach out—sharing the Word, extending personal invitations to others to come to your group, or participating in service projects where your group meets the needs of those in your neighborhood or community. Your Outreach Coordinator will champion and coordinate those efforts to reach outside your group.

GROUP CARE ("INREACH") COORDINATOR _____

_____. Everyone needs a pat on the back once in a while. Therefore, every group also needs a good Inreach Coordinator— someone who oversees caring for the personal needs of group members. That might involve coordinating meals for group members who are sick, making contact with those who have missed group, arranging for birthday/anniversary celebrations for group members, or sending "just thinking of you" notes.

PRAYER COORDINATOR _____.

Your Prayer Coordinator will record and circulate prayer requests to the rest of the group during the week as well as channel any urgent prayer requests to the group that may come up during the week. He or she may also be asked to lead the group in prayer at the close of a session.

SUBGROUP LEADER(S) _____

_____ .

To maximize participation and to have enough time to work through the session, at various points we recommend breaking into smaller subgroups of three or four. Therefore, you'll also need Subgroup Leaders. This is also a great opportunity to develop leaders within the group (who could possibly lead new groups in the future).

CHILD CARE COORDINATOR _____ .

Your Child Care Coordinator will make arrangements to ensure that children are cared for while their parents meet, either at the host's house or at some other agreed-upon location(s). Depending on the makeup of your group, this could be a make-or-break role in ensuring you have a healthy group.

Again, if you don't have volunteers for every role (aside from Leader, Food Coordinator, and Host), that's OK. You may need to think about it first or become more comfortable before making a commitment. What's important is that once you commit to a role, you keep that commitment. If you know you'll miss a session, give the session Leader as much advance notice as possible so your role can be covered.

Whether you volunteer for a role now or want to think things over, take time before the next session to look over the "Group Role Tips" section that begins on the following page. You'll find plenty of useful ideas that will help your group and your role in it (or the role you're considering) be the best they can be.

GROUP ROLE TIPS

FOOD COORDINATOR

1. Sometimes your snack will be a surprise to the rest of the group. Be sure to work closely with your Host and Leader so that the timing of your snacks helps this session be the best it can be.

2. You may also need to arrive a few minutes early to set up the surprise. Set up a time with the Host for your arrival before the meeting.

FOOD COORDINATOR ASSIGNMENTS AND IDEAS

Session 1

There are two snacks you will need to serve for this first session:

- one sweet snack, such as brownies or cookies
- one sour snack, such as salt and vinegar potato chips or lime-flavored tortilla chips

Session 2

This week's snack is also an activity. Your group will be making faces—their own—with the items you supply. Supply enough bagel halves for everyone in the group to have one (bread slices can be substituted but will tear much more easily), cream cheese, peanut butter, and as many of the following as possible:

- grated and baby carrots
- bean sprouts
- raisins
- cherry or grape tomatoes
- olive slices
- cucumber slices
- chocolate chips
- thin ropes of licorice
- mini-marshmallows
- any other small foods you think would be helpful

Note also the "Extra Impact" activity in the margin. Discuss with your Leader whether you'll do this as a group.

Session 3

Ask group members to bring "strange" food items from other cultures. Ask everyone what he or she is bringing beforehand. Make sure at least one especially strange food item is brought—bring it yourself if you need to. Be sure also to have enough of each snack for everyone to sample a given food.

Keep your snacks out at least until the end of your "Taste and See" time. You'll be coming back to it after you first enjoy the snacks group members choose.

Session 4

Bring chips and soda for this session, but make sure it's *flat* soda. Take the lid off your soda a few days in advance (but still keep it in the fridge!) so that the soda is flat when you serve it during the session.

Session 5

This session's surprise food element is water. Serve any other snack you like, but arrange to have two pitchers of water available for the group:

• One pitcher will contain spring water.

• The other pitcher will contain salt water or quinine (tonic) water. (The latter is available at most supermarkets and better conveys the "bitter water" in this session's Scripture passage.)

Make sure there's enough of both kinds of water to serve everyone, and make sure you remember which pitcher is which! If you use bottled quinine water, be sure to keep the bottle hidden from the rest of the group until it's time to serve them.

Session 6

This session's snack is trail mix. You may want to provide a couple of different types of trail mix for your group in case anyone has peanut allergies or simply wants a better dietary choice.

Session 7

You'll need to provide the following:

- mint ice cream for the group
- breath-mint strips for the group—the quick-dissolving kind

The latter "snack" will not be served until "Touching Your World," so be sure to keep your breath strips handy for that time (and preferably hidden until it's time to give them out).

Session 8

Be sure to have an especially attractive snack for this week's session. Chocolate-covered strawberries, cheesecake...your call. The trick here is that you'll want people to be able to look at your snack for at least 10 minutes before they're allowed to eat it. Put it in the middle of the room, if possible, and let people lick their chops. Coordinate the when and how of serving this snack with your Leader and Host.

Thanks again for all your work in making this a successful study!

HOST

1. Before your group gets together, make sure the environment for your session is just right. Is the temperature in your home or meeting place comfortable? Is there enough lighting? Are there enough chairs for everyone? Can they be arranged in a way that everyone's included? Is your bathroom clean and "stocked"? Your home doesn't need to win any awards; just don't let anything be a distraction from your time together.

2. Once your session's started, do what you can to keep it from being interrupted. When possible, don't answer the phone. Ask people to turn off their cell phones or pagers, if necessary. If your phone number's an emergency contact for someone in the group, designate a specific person to answer the phone so your session can continue to run smoothly.

3. If you're responsible for the supplies for your study, be sure to read through the supplies list before each session. If there's any difficulty in supplying any of the materials, let your Leader know or contact someone else in the group who you know has them. The items required for each session are usually common household items, so most weeks this will be pretty easy. Make sure everything's set up before the group arrives.

4. Be sure also to check out what the Food Coordinator has planned each week. Sometimes the snack is a surprise, so he or she may need your help in *keeping* it a surprise for the rest of the group. Your Food Coordinator may also need to arrive a few minutes early to set up, so be sure to work out a time for his or her arrival before the meeting.

5. And, of course, make your guests feel welcome. That's your number-one priority as Host. Greet group members at the door, and make them feel at home from the moment they enter. Spend a few minutes talking with them after your session. Let them know you see them as people and not just "group members." Thank them for coming as they leave.

OUTREACH COORDINATOR

1. Don't forget: New people are the lifeblood of a group. They will keep things from getting stale and will keep your group outwardly focused—as it should be. Encourage the group to invite others.

2. Don't overlook the power of a personal invitation, even to those who don't know Jesus. Invite people from work or your neighborhood to your group, and encourage other group members to do the same.

3. Take special note of the "Touching Your World" section at the end of each session. The last "weekly challenge" is often an "outreach" assignment that can be done either individually or as a group. Be sure to encourage and follow up with group members who take on these challenges.

4. If group members choose an "outreach" option for their weekly challenge, use part of your closing time together to ask God for help in selecting the right service opportunity and that God would bless your group's efforts. Then spend some time afterward discussing what you'll do next.

5. Consider having an event before you begin your *BibleSense* study (or after you finish it). Give a "no obligation" invite to Christians and non-Christians alike just to have the opportunity to meet the others in your group. Do mention, however, what the group will be studying next so they have an opportunity to consider joining you for your next study. Speak with your Leader before making any plans.

6. As part of your personal prayer time, pray that God would bring new people to the group. Make this a regular part of your group's prayer time as well.

GROUP CARE ("INREACH") COORDINATOR

1. Make a point of finding out more about your group members each week. You should be doing this as a group member, but in your role as Inreach Coordinator, you'll have additional opportunities to use what you learn to better care for those in your group.

2. If a group member has special needs, be sure to contact him or her during the week. If it's something the group can help with, get permission first, and then bring the rest of the group into this ministry opportunity.

3. Find out the special dates in your group members' lives, such as birthdays or anniversaries. Make or bring cards for other group members to sign in advance.

4. If someone in your group is sick, has a baby, or faces some other kind of emergency, you may want to coordinate with the rest of the group to provide meals for that person.

PRAYER COORDINATOR

1. Pray for your group throughout the week, and encourage group members to pray for one another. Keep a prayer list, and try to send out prayer reminders after each session.

2. Be sure to keep your group up to date on any current or earlier prayer requests. Pass on "praise reports" when you have them. Remind them that God not only hears but also *answers* prayer.

3. Remember that the role is called Prayer *Coordinator*, not "Official Pray-er for the Group" (whether that's what your group would prefer or not). At the same time, some members of your group may be uncomfortable praying aloud. If there are several people in your group who don't mind praying, one person could open your prayer time and another close it, allowing others to add prayers in between. Give everyone who wants to pray the opportunity to do so.

4. Prayers don't have to be complex and probably shouldn't be. Jesus himself said, "When you pray, don't babble on and on as people of other religions do. They think their prayers are answered merely by repeating their words again and again" (Matthew 6:7).

5. If some group members are intimidated by prayer, begin prayer time by inviting group members to complete a sentence as they pray. For example, ask everyone to finish the following: "Lord, I want to thank you for..."

6. Don't overlook the power of silent prayer. Don't automatically fill "dead spaces" in your prayer time. God may be trying to do that by speaking into that silence. You might even consider closing a session with a time of silent prayer.

SUBGROUP LEADER(S)

1. These sessions are designed to require a minimum of preparation. Nonetheless, be sure to read over each session and watch the DVD in advance to get comfortable with those sections where you may be responsible for leading a subgroup discussion. Highlight any questions you think are important for your subgroup to spend time on for next session.

2. Try not to have the first or last word on every question (or even most of them). Give everyone the opportunity to participate. At the same time, don't put anyone on the spot. Let subgroup members know they can pass on any question they're not comfortable answering.

3. Keep your subgroup time on track. There are suggested time limits for each section. Encourage good discussion, but don't be afraid to rope 'em back in. If you do decide to spend extra time on a question or activity, consider skipping or spending less time on a later question or activity so you can stay on schedule.

CHILD CARE COORDINATOR

There are several ways you can approach the important issue of child care. Discuss as a group which alternative(s) you'll use.

1. The easiest approach may be for group members to each make their own child care arrangements. Some might prefer this; others may not be able to afford it on their own. If a parent or couple needs financial assistance, see if someone else in the group can help out in this area.

2. If your meeting area is conducive to it, have group members bring their children to the meeting, and have on-site child care available so parents can pay on a child-by-child basis.

3. If most or all of your group members have young children, you could also consider rotating child care responsibilities around the group rather than paying someone else.

4. If there are members in your group who have older children who are mature enough to watch the younger children, pay them to handle your child care. Maybe they can even do their own lesson. If so, Group offers a number of great materials for children of all ages—go to www.group.com to find out more.

5. Check to see if the youth group at your church would be interested in providing child care as a fundraiser.

> **Important:** It is wise to prescreen any potential child care worker, paid or volunteer, who is watching children as part of a church-sanctioned activity (including a home Bible study). Your church may already have a screening process in place that can be utilized for your group. If not, Group's Church Volunteer Central network (www.churchvolunteercentral .com) is a great resource, containing ready-made background-check and parental-consent forms as well as articles and other online resources.